book of days

book of days
Linda France

Smoke

STACK
BOOKS

For Kevin!

never befriend a
woman who writes
haiku

Linda x

Published 2009 by
Smokestack Books
PO Box 408, Middlesbrough TS5 6WA
e-mail : info@smokestack-books.co.uk
www.smokestack-books.co.uk

book of days
Linda France
Cover image: Dave Ward
Author photograph: Karen Melvin
Artwork: Sue Dunne

Printed by
EPW Print & Design Ltd

ISBN 978-0-9560341-3-7
Smokestack Books gratefully
acknowledges the support of
Arts Council England

Smokestack Books is
represented by Inpress Ltd
www.inpressbooks.co.uk

Thanks are due to the editor of island *where 'August' and 'September' were first published.*

for Alec
seed, bloom and fruit

Different Ways of Saying 'Year'

At the beginning of 2006 I set myself the challenge of writing one renga verse every day, alternating three lines and two lines in the manner of the traditional collaborative renga form. I'd charted the months of the year in various projects (*wild*, with artist Birtley Aris, Sand Press, in 2003, and *The Moon & Flowers,* at Chesters Walled Garden, in 2005) so was already investigating the principle of using time and space, literally, as aspects of poetic form. I wanted my year renga to capture the ongoing moment, 365 word pictures to bear witness to my own sense of presence, my aliveness to everyday revelations. Both the form and the practice would act as a discipline to harness the busyness of my thoughts.

Renga dates from 10th century Japan, a culture more familiar than ours with principles of protocol and restraint. Japanese poets would gather and write verses together, often drinking tea or saki for hours at a time. Their traditional subjects were the natural world, love, the moon, shining things and falling things, all phenomena vulnerable to change.

Translated across the centuries from East to West, variations on the theme of renga have been developed by contemporary writers and artists drawn to the purity and presence contained within the practice. It is above all a practical art – like zen archery or calligraphy – where the nuances of the process are as vital as the outcome.

I have been participating in and leading rengas for nearly a decade, enjoying the way it allows me to bring together what I know of poetry and of Buddhism, usually by reminding me just how much ground there is still to be covered.

Ordinarily a renga involves a group of people gathered together for five or six hours, led by a master, who brings the first verse, a three line *hokku* (the origin of the haiku form), evoking the season the renga itself is taking place in. All the writers compose alternating two and three line verses, a round for each, on a particular theme, according to the chosen schema, responding to, but departing from, the preceding verse. The master selects each linking verse, perhaps suggesting changes or the combining of two different poets' verses. This results in a twenty-verse sequence, like beads on a string, each one a small world of its own. The effect is non-linear, in terms of narrative, and non-rational, with no consistent 'voice' or tense, qualities it shares with post-modernism. However in renga the sense is held in the awareness informing the text, the openness to experience and its translation into words by, with or from the participants. A renga is a peculiarly ablative form, a mode generally considered of lesser importance in our anthropocentric, nominative world.

My experiment with the *book of days* required me to break away from the comfort of familiarity. In the absence of fellow collaborators I was continually thrown back on my own resources, my own viewpoint. I missed the freshness of someone else's words, the shock and stimulus of the new. Borrowing the usual inconsistencies of voice, I allowed myself to play with pronouns, the traditional writer's device of mask and mirror. My friends, my daily walks, the weather, my own small dramas, everything I saw, heard and read, became my collaborators and I needed to be master of them all. I worked mostly intuitively, letting the thread of my days carry me through. What I made of my world, inside and out, became the schema and I had to trust it would allow sufficient variety and flow – 'link and shift' – in the spirit of a collaborative renga. Occasionally the rigour of staying open enough to let a verse come and find me would elude me and last thing at night I had to re-run my day and wilfully try to find the verse hidden in whatever had unfolded hour by hour.

An unusual mixture of inclusiveness towards all the possibilities that might arise and discrimination in the selection of what to settle on is necessary to write renga and it is this quality of mind that continues to fascinate me. There is something paradoxical about the place of virtual surrender, the dis-inhibition and lack of self-consciousness the imagination must inhabit, while also needing to be watchful as a snake waiting for its prey. It is poised and dynamic, centred and open, in the flow of things.

On the page, the *book of days* can be what every reader wants it to be – calendar, diary, mandala, litany, inventory, touchstone, or some other facility I can't see in it yet. I have divided it into months, introduced by Sue Dunne's beautiful ceramic fragments: reliefs created by casting flower, leaf and branch; all found in the woods and hedgerows, where we live in Northumberland, as a year unfolds.

The seasons are shifting before our eyes, no longer neatly divided into spring, summer, autumn and winter. For me, renga is one way of paying attention to the world, natural and man-made, acknowledging its mystery and significance and seeking balance and perspective in a time out of kilter.

Linda France   2009

January

New year
old dust
new broom

    next door's bonfire
    black smoke spiralling

my sons – the pleasure
of having them both
under the same roof

    in the midnight sky where there should be
    a meteor shower – freezing fog

on the station platform
little beads of snow
as I pace up and down

    pylons fizz in the mist
    the ghost of Stagshaw Fair

halfway there
remembering I've forgotten
my walking boots

    I try to describe
    an invisible elephant

which half of me
is telling which half
of you the truth?

    I brush the cobwebs from the corners
    and wash the soot off the shelves

a day with three owls
in it – paper,
feather, stone

sadness: not knowing
where your tears end and mine begin

all day long the wind
argues with the house,
the trees, me

hard to tell where the light is –
in the frost or in the moon

over two miles away
the sound of the traffic
cleaves the stillness

between them the rabbits and the moles
are turning my garden into a battlefield

a rough-haired terrier
with empty eyes
tries to follow me home

everyone in the coffee shop
younger than me

in the Turkish
we exercise
our talking muscles

the scrape of the shovel
as I fill three buckets with coal

inside Abdullah Ibrahim
is playing – outside
birds are singing

since waking up I wanted to cry –
in the dark of the shrine room I do

to see what is true
and hold it
with kindness

she lifted her arms and pretended
to dance like a lemur

first tips of snowdrops
under the hawthorn
rain falling

how many candles burned away
as we sat at the table and talked?

tapping enough to wake me
a door or a drum
my beating heart

I want to dive into those patches
of sky that are the brightest blue

lichen on the rowan tree
tinged golden
by lengthening sun

two magpies stripe icy morning light
joy! joy! joy!

our nervous spoons skate
across the dark shine
of one crème brûlée

February

opening the door
to the scent of daffodils

a glimpse
of the woodpecker
its wide green back

the waitress eats an apple
admires my scarlet coat

the picture of you
when you were four
the scar on your lip

the next day I was still
thinking about her belly button

purple in the pond
like petals that disappear
when you touch them

quoted on the secondhand bookjacket –
the sweet delusion of the flesh

for his 79th birthday
I bring him John Coltrane
and Thelonius Monk Live

what's the appeal of North?
she asks – her favourite's West

after the shiatsu
my shoulders
sleep in Chinese

*the human heart in conflict
with itself*: he makes it sound appealing

I translate a demon
called Brother Magpie
into a new friend

on St Valentine's Eve I find
a heart-shaped stone in the middle of the road

hear a horse
behind you
that isn't there

in the village she sees a bear as tall
as she is, clasping a fishing rod, even taller

all the naked people
of Newcastle
stacked like shrimps

someone else's self-pity
easier to spot than my own

a touch of cowboy about the way
the man in the Post Office
counts out his dollars

turn that word 'awareness' into a room
you can walk into, make a home in

inside and outside
a monthful of weather
in a single day

blue sky reflected in peaty water –
a golden mirror

red in the rowan tree
bird not berry
lesser spotted

throw me a bone
to feed the dog of my heart

in Warsaw
one man kept on
playing the piano

    because I know you'll be reading this
    I can't say how much I wanted you then

inscribe 240 poems
on a small gourd –
then what?

    coming home to snow and stars,
    my electric blanket, *Late Junction*

it's been six months
and no one's collected
the shiny Ferrari

March

already on the radio they're arguing
about when exactly spring begins

woken early
by a woodpecker
drilling the mortar

I have to break the ice in the water butt
all the orchids frosted and dead

even in the city
the enchantment
of snowfall

today's small things – a white feather
holly berries, caterpillar, wren

three hours later
those cock pheasants
still sparring

I try to soothe her
but she'd rather worry

raindrops are pearls
set in silver
on the filigree birch

one idea of heaven
Athol Brose in a big bowl

I choose a diamond button
thinking of your parents
their sixty years together

lost in translation
lover and *brother*

fire's on before noon
a scarf of zero
wrapped round the house

  a woman whose name isn't Lola
  makes films about snow

his birthday eclipse
hidden in the blur
over Byker Bridge

  under the yellow city lights
  she's taking three shadows for a walk

hot chips
on the sea front
salty breeze

  she was bleaching into paper
  warm milk, wheatfield, wet sand

I love walls
that lean, ivy
that breaks free

  collecting winkles smashed by gulls
  their silky chambers exposed

frogs pretend
to be leaves as leaves
pretend to be frogs

  as if the robin sang
  just for me

the coffee guy
spills the beans
about Jehovah

  the heart urchin I tried
  to save crushed in my pocket

they found each other
in the rain –
she knew they would

    green plover, lapwing, peewit –
    why does a bird need three different names?

halfway between our houses
we climb the hill
to Heavenfield

    the day his father died
    the year's first daffodils

a theatreful
of vaginas –
us in the upper circle

    when the sun goes dark I'm horizontal
    breathing in orange, geranium, petit grain

more than just the taste
of sambar, dosa takes you
back to Kerala

    the young monk is happy
    doesn't know what day it is

April

keeping my head down
picking my way
between mud and puddles

    all of a sudden your voice
    in the headphones, the suck of my breath

he draws rivers
like streams of stars
names them

    her daughter's eyes are her eyes
    her wide smile

he's telling me
I should be grateful
for Margaret Thatcher

    no water for a bath
    rinsing my teeth from the kettle

the old woman
in the jacuzzi
ENDURANCE on her cozzie

    she knew she was healed
    when she stopped crying when she came

roundabout daffs
masquerade
as spring flowers

    I wonder when it was
    I started liking night best

a year later
we're back in the woods
and everything's different

see the black-tailed stoat chase the rabbit
a strange, ancient game

around midnight
Julia's moon
single malt

I scoop up all the little white bones
where the owl pellet rotted away

Thai New Year
magenta orchids
on the shrine

everything she thinks about
she's already thought about

the new door blows
shut locking me
and my big ideas in

your orgasms are the colour
of a chestnut mare

floral crosses and hearts
by the dark stain
on the switchback road

the teacups in the boot rattling
like lovesick birds

saying yes
too quick
is a sort of lie

listening to his music in the dark
hard to believe he isn't there too

love in the beginning
love in the middle
love in the end

the quad's magnolia stellata
is a clean page, all the students back

awake in the night
wind buffeting
starless dark

under sodium lights blossom
is dream-coloured, bewitching

Hobbesian man
roams the streets
glitter in his hair

I am a woman
with too many books

the smell of him
in the car does something
difficult to my throat

8 a.m. turning on the radio
the first word *anxiety*

May

a massacre
and a mutiny
for Mayday

    the wooden slats of the sauna
    burning lines in my back

in the café Louis Primo
wrenches her where?
how many years? twelve?

    black Galloway on the fell
    white heart on its left flank

every time you come
home you've grown
more into yourself

    finches drink and bathe
    among leaf and shadow

Scots pine
at the end of the drive
anemones at the top

    we worry about drinking
    Starbucks coffee in the sun

and in the end
it's easy
saying what I need

    a fat black millipede articulates
    itself across the bathroom floor

he tried to be cheerful
to trick himself
into thinking he was

where is the stranger, the reader,
in the half-light of the buried life?

a dream
of a pregnant belly
mine, happy

getting what you want doesn't
solve anything the monk laughs

I want to have written
everyone else's poem
but my own

every leaf on the birch tree
ten thousand wings

books disagree
about its call
tsee-too or *zip-zip-zip-chittityk*

the turbulence makes her
regret her unusual breakfast

the drum does it
wakes him up
makes the beat sting

the only two peregrine fledglings
in the city keep close to the cathedral

from Tintin's birthplace
I carry home
a cast-off boxbox

he's mowed every verge
a mile's radius from the house

your favourite nun
suggests dignity
an antidote to lust

the cow charges at me, wet-nostrilled,
full-uddered, protecting her unborn calf

her song
touches me
under my skin

how to choose between two vases
each as beautiful as the other?

Rosie mows the grass
between showers
quick as it grows

my tree from the British Library –
'The Tree of Knowledge': no apples yet

did I really wake up
with the taste of Durex
and grapefruit, ruby-red?

north of midnight
crescent moon comes true

a story of snake venom
reminds her of Rilke –
his roses, their thorns

June

Marilyn Monroe's 80th birthday
men in skirts pretend to be peacocks

she sits on the lawn
shy of my eyes
I see myself in hers

we watch the wheel at Killhope
the three of us, glossy and intense

they wonder if
the dog's blind,
see his lostness

sometimes it's my hurt
that speaks, craving comfort

in sunshine and shade
we build a platform
for summer

she sways gently as she plays
squeezing the bag under her elbow

a lone oystercatcher
soars calling
over the Co-op car park

flowers of the dunes:
bloody cranesbill, burnet rose

sometimes cleaning
the pond is just
cleaning the pond

and then the mower blade
slices through the black cord

you will find poetry
nowhere unless you bring
some of it with you

    I imagine you sitting by your window
    watching the birds

he says he'll write
from the swamps
of Okefenokee

    sleeping in a different bed
    I wake up in a different skin

opposite each other
they both think
about metal

    even in the pouring rain
    we keep on writing

a sign
from nowhere:
House of Recovery

    I find her in a wheelchair smoking
    her first cigarette for two weeks

at solstice you float
a solar-powered firefly
on the dark pond

    after her nap she writes
    a short essay about death

we dismantle it
rebuild it
dismantle it again

    the woman with hennaed hair
    speaks slowly about her lost child

the maze
is punctuated
with water, steel

    crimson sequins, chiffon –
    the drag queen's third change

pale blue meconopsis
fragile on tall stems
bulging yellow eyes

    a dead fledgling in the storm
    canopy of dripping leaves

going slowly
to catch
the healing

    her touch on my hips
    makes them ripple, arch

whose voice
do I hear singing
about horses?

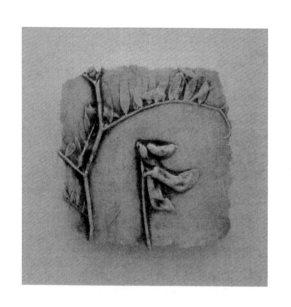

July

dragonfly and snake
your mouth smiling and smiling

perjink? fankles?
she needs him
to translate

the pine cone on your mantelpiece
both seed and fruit

my hands sticky
from recycling
sorting white from green

skystruck the reservoir
is the colour of coral

blinded by desire
the pickpocket only
spots a saint's pockets

two wrens flirt
on the gable end

half a margharita
a plate of tapas
and you're in Mexico

unpicking that stitch behind my navel
that keeps me tight, apart

your strong hands –
I see now
how small they are

the rabbi said we're all
still in kindergarten

last night's moon
a woman's face
mouth open

    after a morning recording deaths
    coffee and lemon drizzle cake

in front of us
the lawn fills
with white doves

    breakfast with Leonard Cohen
    sun singing my skin awake

learning a new language
she checks her smile
in the mirror

    half a daytime moon
    ice in a glass of blue

the shadow of a tern
on the deck
of the boat

    white stripes on my feet
    where my sandals have been

nothing prettier
than a woman
with dimples

    she brings mangetout
    from the allotment, two potatoes

Mary Magdelene's Day –
patron saint
of pharmacists, hairdressers

    five of us in the room
    five different ways of saying 'year'

PMT dosed
with sepia
cuttlefish ink

> I mislay half an hour
> a whole moon

massaging her feet
as if he had at least
four hands

> all the boats have the same name –
> *Walker Bay*

throwing away
my mother's mirror
the shattering

> the drive north is a river
> and returning

the truth is
I am easily
confused

> pins and needles
> playing the clutch

August

after the meditation
she is rainbowed
and tearless

  rain suddenly
  unfamiliar, miraculous

the first dragonfly
a dance of yellow
metallic green

  she traces the thread between
  my ear and my heart

after three lines
you start
telling lies

  I wish the road
  were shorter, straighter

count the times
what I call reality
contradicts itself

  loosestrife sheds its purple
  in the estuary dunes

I fill my pocket
with sea glass
rubbed smooth

  poisonous plants like women's names –
  belladonna, nicotiana, artemisia

she wants to mark
her cracked places
with gold lacquer

the glorious twelfth
your sapphire eyes

can't sleep
you write
but happy

Hodgkin's *Venetian Views*
inspire me to reframe my own

how to build
a rose arch
roseless?

a green draught
through the sunroof

overnight a spider's
wrapped the wing
mirror in webs

woken by a bittern
tooting the bassoon

I come home
to your fire
your food

four bottles of speciality ale
emptied in an evening, *Fursty Ferret*

there's so much
even in one moment
I don't understand

twice the deer and I
startle each other

just when you thought
you were done
with suffering

she burns candles in my ears
splits them open, wax on wax

August dust
is the worst dust
dirty with what's over

the slow worm quick
and bronze across our path

loving needs you
to leave
your mind behind

mango juice so thick
the straw stands up

the note
by her bedside
the beat of my name

Bergman's *Autumn Sonata*
the women's faces in knots

at what point
does a choice
become a chain?

September

I lose myself in the story
find myself there all along

you text me
Chet Baker
my phone alight

the dark horse has cheeks
of suede and a mischievous tongue

hammering in my head –
am I being rebuilt
or demolished?

Lolo's flamenco drum
the sound of its vowels: *cajon*

all I can fit
in my mind
is the moon

tawny owl you say
nuthatch, blackbird, robin

I read her face
a long glass
of clear water

from the train the sea
is even more beautiful

cygnets as big
and hungry
as their mother

left forefinger and thumb
the letter 'L'

I remember
to water the gardenia
forget my keys

    you juggle a spinning ball
    on a knife between your teeth

lightning flickers
off the corner
of my reading glasses

    Japanese anemones let loose
    their pale pink petals

your small noises
on the rug
the fire's crackle

    Miss Dolan's Delight
    on the lap of *The Bishop*

sky a book
of changes
open over water

    when he says *Love your enemy*
    it stops being theatre

the taste
of disappointment
four day old bread

    birdsong suggests an open throat
    at least the possibility of love

a cold sore
means no kissing
no being kissed

    illusion: sunlight, willow
    a river flowing upstream

the comfort
of blanket stitch
Pure New Wool

> your silence filled
> with what I can't give

two people
with the same name
a different loss

> the poem you wrote me then
> a surprise in the dark auditorium

at the Cumberland Arms
her green scarf
her pint of gold

> the mushrooms grow taller
> their caps thin to cinders

I talk
to no-one
all day

> is what we are making
> a bowl of clay
> to pour ourselves in?

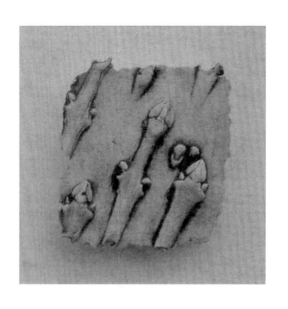

October

after three days of reading, silence
the supermarket is a sort of hell

how did it happen
that students should
look so glamorous?

you show me your sunburn
a nude by Lucian Freud

this is poetry
I am not this I
you are not that you

the ghosts of all the lives
you ever said no to

aqueduct – always
a beautiful word
especially in liquid light

in this part of the world
they call you *duck*

a boat
heaped full
of sunset glass

LO
VE

a Japanese girl looks up
electronic translations –
piecemeal, fistful, red letter day

no, we couldn't shoe
our running horse

sometimes only
the water of life
will do

    my burrito, my baby
    you knickerbocker glory

her son makes
a rocket
of his mother's ashes

    the vihara's 25 years old
    and she's seen 23 of them

travelling back
to a county
I keep on losing

    beech branch, quiver
    the nut brown squirrel teasing

woodsmoke
from the chimney
spiriting us home

    three days at Lumb Bank
    a mirage months-long

pink champagne
fizzing, birthdayish
on my tongue

    she reads their talking
    Dutch like a signpost

hanging washing
collecting pinecones
fetching coal

    the sweet smell
    of evening, blown leaves

whenever I dream
of you we're in
a very deep room

    he brings her a square
    of his favourite viyella shirt

they move together
eel-like
among museum stones

    breathless on the phone
    needing more than air

the lake's grey –
heron feathers
flying into winter

    you rise to the fall
    of water, its roar, your smile

my new hat's
shocking turquoise
warms my ears

    we map the world
    in football teams, Champions League

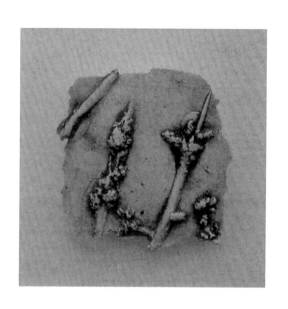

November

an umbrella
of Tibetan rhubarb
over the garden wall

    three women for whom
    sunlight is enough

moon's a cat's eye
keeping me on the right side
of the road

    burning the goddess
    we all get burned

look after her
he tells
his mother's new squeeze

    you know – *sleepkissing*
    walking with your lips

poems are like dreams:
in them you put what
you don't know you know

    a wild pink kite dances
    in the glittering eye of the sea

flying to the fiords
in search of whales
an early start

    we unpack our suitcases –
    mothers and lovers and sons

everywhere I look
is the colour
of her hair

a flock of wagtails hop
across leaf-skinned water

three-quarters asleep
I read
mystical rabbits

at his city flat
outside spills indoors

soft with lichen
the old wall interrupted
by a Victorian letterbox

after the watershed
we have no language

I paint my lips
hawthorn berry
brake light, Rothko

in their soldiers' colours
they gather after the shoot

I fish leaves
out of the pond
a smell of rot

the boys fit in an extra drink
while the girls eat Haagen-Dazs

the radio makes her cry
the owl calling
always in B flat

a butterfly waking up
on a woman sleeping

for one night
I am Francesca
damned for love

and so they come into
each other's hands

the next day
banjo and mandolin
still twanging

    her new ring – the effect
    kitchen unit, gravestone

late for the train
as if not wanting
the day to end

    he lists his ingredients
    feeding her taste by taste

the simplicity
of walking
rosehips on bare branches

    if I rearrange my rooms
    will I be rearranged?

December

a child, her suitcase –
loss locked in
her face

    thank god for the alphabet!
    each letter perfect and in the right order

already she's dreading
Christmas
all her wishes

    I debate the ethics
    of buying him poker chips

an invisible woman
making everything
visible around her

    you send me the moon
    a circle of careful words

she can't find the book
he gave her –
worse than losing him

    your kiss in the dark
    the taste of tea

shape of a woman
in serpentine marble
caught and freed

    where the stem carries
    the flower – inflorescence

why does it matter
whether you use blue biro
or black ink?

a jolt of electricity
the first time I met you

celtic knots
flash
in her ear lobes

across the border
driving in a different language

first thing
two deer
snow on the hills

frost creeps on cat paws
down to the loch

a man asks
is pain
one of the five senses?

branches burn
like bones

a hawk's cry
casts ripples
in still air, water

walking to morning meditation –
a path of stars

two flutes
more beautiful
than one

lifting earth and holding sky
Larry chi kungs on the lawn

are you waiting
for time to show you
some better thoughts?

Christmas Eve – silverfish
in the jigsaw box

everything dead
sealed in beads
of ice and clouds of fog

can't see the edges
of the road, the next turn

all the letters
on my keyboard
worn away

never befriend a woman
who writes haiku

polishing the gift
her mother's silver
from 1976

what I want for you
is what I want for me

blown open
the year
the last day.